S T E C K ◼ V A U G H N

WRITING
FOR COMPETENCY

W9-AGA-103

James W. Beers, Ph.D.
College of William and Mary

J. Thomas Gill, Jr., Ph.D.
University of Virginia

Steck-Vaughn
Company

A Subsidiary of National Education Corporation

- P.O. Box 2028 Austin, Texas 78768

Photography Credits

Cover: David C. Mackenzie
Inside Photos: David C. Mackenzie

ISBN 0-8114-1844-8

2 3 4 5 6 7 8 9 0 AS 92 91 90 89 88

Contents

To the Student

Writing

Does your school district require that you write an essay in order to proceed to the next grade or to graduate? You may be nervous about taking such a writing test. You may feel that you don't write well enough to pass a test.

The best way to become comfortable with writing is to write. The more you write, the easier it will be. If you feel very nervous about writing, begin to keep a journal. Write one sentence every day. Write whatever you feel like writing. Don't worry about spelling or punctuation. Just write. If you don't have anything to write about, just copy something that you have read in a book or a magazine. Or write a list of things you need to do. Or write about how you feel about writing. Then start writing several sentences. Then more and more. You don't have to show your journal to anyone. It is just for you. Go back and read what you have written. You will see that you can write!

Practice writing whenever you have a chance. Write letters to your relatives or friends. Write a letter to the editor of your newspaper. Write a letter to a movie star. Write a letter to the author of a book you read. Write, write, write, then write some more!

Writing for a test, however, will be somewhat different than the writing you do every day. You will need to plan and organize carefully. You will need to watch your time. This book can help you. It will give you an easy-to-follow, step-by-step approach that will help you take a writing test—successfully!

The Writing Test

Content The writing assignment will be brief. It will ask you to form an opinion about an issue or situation familiar to you. You will be expected to write a composition that clearly explains and defends your point of view. You will not need any special knowledge or information to respond to the topic. A typical assignment, for example, might ask you to describe the effects of the automobile on modern life.

Scoring Your composition will be scored "holistically." This means that your composition will be judged on its overall effectiveness. A few misspellings or a few usage errors will not cause your composition to fail, although too many of each might. What is most important is how well you stick to the topic and how well you support your topic with good examples.

The POWER Writing Program

Steck-Vaughn's *WRITING FOR COMPETENCY* is a good place to begin preparing for a writing test. Writing seems difficult to do. But by giving you a step-by-step approach to writing a composition, this book gives you the POWER to succeed. In fact, we call our program the POWER Program. Each step— from how to begin your composition to how to end it—is spelled out for you. **P** stands for PLAN, **O** for ORGANIZE, **W** for WRITE, **E** for EVALUATE, and **R** for REVISE. Look at the chart on the next page. It summarizes the POWER Writing Program.

P	Plan	**Step 1** Read the writing assignment.
		Step 2 List your ideas.
O	Organize	**Step 3** Group your ideas. Name each group.
		Step 4 Expand your groups. Put your groups in order.
W	Write	**Step 5** Write the introduction.
		Step 6 Write the body.
		Step 7 Write the conclusion.
E	Evaluate	**Step 8** Evaluate your composition.
R	Revise	Make the changes that are needed.

Study the POWER Steps until they come easily to you. If you can do that, you are well on your way to being prepared for the writing test. You can practice the POWER Steps in the section called "Practicing for the Test." You can choose from a number of practice writing assignments in that section. You will also find a Writing Guide that helps you remember the step-by-step method of writing a successful composition.

The Writing Guide also helps you time your writing. As you become more familiar with the POWER Steps and the actual method of writing a composition becomes easier, you should begin to pay attention to how much time it takes you to write. You may have only 45 minutes to complete a writing test. Spend your time wisely!

You may be surprised to find that we recommend you spend most of your time not actually writing your composition, but planning and organizing your writing. In fact, if you plan and organize your writing well, the actual writing of your composition should take less time. The Writing Guide you find in "Practicing for the Test" will help you pace yourself. Each POWER Step in the Writing Guide has a handy time reminder to keep you on track. Practice your timing with the practice writing assignments until you can write an effective composition in 45 minutes.

If you have trouble remembering any POWER Step, go back and review it. The Summaries are a quick way to review if you just need refreshing. Skim the Summaries in each step to find the important ideas and the many hints for writing an effective composition found in this book, WRITING FOR COMPETENCY.

Reading the Writing Assignment

PLANNING

A. Instruction

Suppose you have to take a test to show how well you can write. It might be called a Writing Sample. It might be called a Proficiency Test. It might be called a Basic Skills Test. Whatever it is called, it usually begins with a **writing assignment**. Let's look at a typical writing assignment:

> Many people dream of owning a car. In some ways, owning a car can give you new opportunities. In other ways, owning a car can make your life more difficult.
>
> Write a composition of about 200 words describing how owning a car might affect your life. Describe the good effects, the bad effects, or both. Be specific. Use examples to support your points.

It is very important to read the writing assignment carefully. You have to know exactly *what* you are supposed to write about. Where does the writing assignment tell you *what* to write? Look at these words in the second paragraph: *describing how owning a car might affect your life*. This is the *what*; this is your **topic**. It tells you what you are supposed to write about.

There is more useful information in the writing assignment.

> ▼ There is **background** about the topic.
> ▼ There are **instructions** on how to write about the topic.

Let's look at the same writing assignment again. Read it carefully. Notice that the topic is circled for you.

> Many people dream of owning a car. In some ways, owning a car can give you new opportunities. In other ways, owning a car can make your life more difficult.
>
> Write a composition of about 200 words (describing how) (owning a car might affect your life.) Describe the good effects, the bad effects, or both. Be specific. Use examples to support your points.

What **background** are you given in this writing assignment? Look at the part that is in color. It introduces you to the topic. It gives you some ideas about the topic. It helps you understand the topic. This is the background part of the writing assignment. Think about it before you write.

What are the **instructions** for this writing assignment? Look at the underlined words in the second paragraph. These are the instructions. They tell you how to write your composition. You are given four important instructions:

1. You should write about 200 words.
2. You should describe the good effects, or the bad effects, or both.
3. You should be specific.
4. You should use examples to make each point.

Every word in the writing assignment is there to help you. The **topic** tells you what to write about. The **background** gives you ideas about the topic. The **instructions** tell you how to write.

SUMMARY

Always look for three things when you read a writing assignment:

1. the topic
2. the background
3. the instructions

B. Practice

1. Read the writing assignment below. The background is in color.

   ▼ Circle the topic.

   ▼ Underline the instructions.

   ▼ Copy the topic and the instructions on the lines below.

   ▼ Look back at the model on page 10 if you need help.

> Skateboards are very popular, but many people think they are dangerous.
>
> In a composition of about 200 words, explain your own opinion of skateboards. Be specific. Give examples to support your view.

Topic _____

_____

_____

_____

Instructions _____

_____

_____

_____

_____

_____

_____

_____

2. Read the writing assignment below. The background is in color.

▼ Circle the topic.

▼ Underline the instructions.

▼ Write the topic and the instructions on the lines below. You may use your own words or add extra words to what is already there.

In our society today, people may move every few years. By moving often, people can experience different places and climates. They can also meet many new people and make new friends. But some people prefer to stay in one place all their lives and never move far from home. They feel secure in a place they know and like to keep the same friends and neighbors.

Write a composition of about 200 words stating whether you think it is better to stay in one place or to move often and live different places. Be specific. Give examples to support your view.

Topic _____

_____

_____

_____

Instructions _____

_____

_____

_____

3. Read the writing assignment below. The background is in color.

▼ Circle the topic.

▼ Underline the instructions.

▼ Write the topic and the instructions in your own words. Do not look back!

▼ Check what you have written by rereading the assignment.

> Professional football players often earn large salaries. They earn much more than police, fire fighters, or office workers do. Yet they work shorter hours and for only part of the year. Some people think football players are paid too much for just playing games. Other people think that football players should earn as much as movie stars and TV stars do because they provide entertainment.
>
> Write a composition of about 200 words stating whether you think football players are paid too much or not. Explain your view. Give specific examples about football and about other kinds of work.

Topic _____

_____

Instructions _____

_____

_____

▼ **Answers** to Step 1 Practice Exercises are on page 123.

▼ **Extra Practice**. Use Step 1 Review on pages 80–81 for extra help.

C. Application

As you work through this book, you will be asked to use each step you learn in the POWER Writing Program. You will have a chance to review and practice every stage of putting a composition together. In each Part C exercise, you will apply what you have learned toward creating a composition of your own. When you finish the book, you will have put together your own composition, step by step.

In Step 1, you learned to read the writing assignment. You learned to look for three things: the topic, the background, and the instructions. Now you can apply what you know.

Read Writing Assignment 1 and Writing Assignment 2. Choose one of them. Choose the one you would most like to write about.

▼ Circle the topic in the writing assignment you choose.

▼ Underline the instructions.

▼ Write the topic and the instructions on the lines on the next page.

Writing Assignment 1

> The telephone was invented by Alexander Graham Bell in 1876. Today, almost everyone in the United States has access to a telephone. Telephones have helped us keep in touch with one another. But telephones can also be a nuisance.
>
> Write an essay of about 200 words stating whether you think telephones are a help or a nuisance. Be specific. Give examples to support your view.

Writing Assignment 2

> Motorcycles are popular for recreation and fun. They are also a cheap way to travel. But in recent years, many people have died in motorcycle accidents. Some people think motorcycles are unsafe and should be strictly regulated.
>
> Write a composition of about 200 words, giving your own opinion of motorcycles. Do you feel they are hazardous or beneficial? Be specific. Give examples to support your view.

Topic _____

_____

_____

_____

Instructions _____

_____

_____

_____

_____

_____

_____

Note: This is the beginning of your own composition.
BE SURE TO SAVE THIS PAGE!

Listing Your Ideas

PLANNING

A. Instruction

You have read the writing assignment. You have identified the topic, the background, and the instructions. Now what? Now comes the most important step in planning your composition—listing your ideas.

For this step, write down all the ideas you can think of about the writing assignment. You will use this list of ideas to put together your composition.

How do you list all your ideas? Read. Think. Write. Follow the steps below:

▼ READ the assignment until you are sure you understand it.

▼ THINK about the assignment you've read and the things it asks you to discuss.

▼ WRITE the ideas that come to mind—as many as you can.

Remember, a good composition needs good ideas and plenty of them. The best ideas you get may not be the first ideas you get. Don't stop with two or three ideas. If you list only a few ideas, you're stuck with those. If you make a long list of ideas, you can pick and choose the best. So keep thinking!

While you are thinking, don't worry about how good the ideas are. Just write them all down. You will go back and review them later and decide which ones you can use. At this point, you want to write down *everything* you think of about the assignment.

Remember: the *longer* your list of ideas, the *stronger* your writing will be.

SUMMARY

When listing your ideas, remember: **READ**
↓
THINK
↓
WRITE

Repeat these steps as often as you need to.

The longer your list of ideas, the stronger your composition will be.

Let's look at how one student went about listing her ideas. Lynn read the writing assignment below. She circled the topic. She underlined the instructions. (The background is in color.)

Many people dream of owning a car. In some ways, owning a car can give you new opportunities. In other ways, owning a car can make your life more difficult.

Write a composition of about 200 words (describing how) (owning a car might affect your life.) Describe the good effects, the bad effects, or both. Be specific. Use examples to support your points.

Now follow Lynn's thoughts as she lists her ideas.

Lynn's Thoughts	**Lynn's Idea List**
"Hmm, owning a car. What do I think about owning a car? Well, my friends would be so impressed. A car of my own! They would know where I was just by seeing my car."	*impress friends* *sense of identity*
"I wouldn't have to ask my parents for the car. And I wouldn't have to ask them to pick me up or take me places if they needed the car."	*freedom* *won't have to ask parents for their car* *won't have to ride with others*
"I would have a way to get to work—I could have a job!"	*can have a job*

"I could take my friends out. We could do all kinds of things together!"

take friends places

"It would be great to go out for rides, especially in the country where there are hills.'

go out for rides

"But I would have to pay for gas."

cost of gas

"Let's see. I have nine ideas listed. I can't think of anything else. Maybe I need to take a break."

After a few minutes . . .

"Well, gas wouldn't be the only cost. I would have to pay for insurance. And maybe tires or a battery sometime."

cost of insurance
cost of parts

"But it would be great to have my very own car. I would take care of it myself. I would take good care of it."

take pride in car
take good care of it

SUMMARY

When you've listed as many ideas as you can, rest a bit. Then look at your list. Does it have enough strong ideas to work with?

"I think a car would be fantastic. I would feel independent. But I would also feel responsible."

sense of independence
sense of responsibility

Lynn reread the writing assignment. She looked over her list again. She had a good list of ideas on which to base her composition. She had completed Step 2.

B. Practice

1. Read the writing assignment below. The topic is circled. The instructions are underlined. The background is in color. Three ideas are already written to help you begin.

▼ Write as many more ideas as you can. Add at least six ideas. Remember, the longer your list, the better.

> Skateboards are very popular, but many people think they are dangerous.
>
> In a composition of about 200 words, (explain your own opinion of skateboards.) Be specific. Give examples to support your view.

Idea List

good exercise

develop balance

chance of injury

2. Remember to list only ideas about the topic. Avoid ideas that might lead in another direction.

▼ Read the idea list that Jeff wrote for the topic circled in the box below.

▼ Cross out the three ideas that are not about the topic.

▼ Add other ideas to make a longer list.

In our society today, people may move every few years. By moving often, people can experience different places and climates. They can also meet many new people and make new friends. But some people prefer to stay in one place all their lives and never move far from home. They feel secure in a place they know and like to keep the same friends and neighbors.

Write a composition of about 200 words (stating whether you think it is better to stay in one place or to move often and live different places.) Be specific. Give examples to support your view.

Idea List

more experiences	learn way around new area
change schools	music
movies	pack up everything
keep same friends	new things to see and do
books	new friends
may have new climate	

3. Read the writing assignment below. The background is in color.

▼ List your ideas. Remember, the longer the list, the stronger your composition will be.

Professional football players often earn large salaries. They earn much more than police, fire fighters, or office workers do. Yet they work shorter hours and for only part of the year. Some people think football players are paid too much for just playing games. Other people think that football players should earn as much as movie stars and TV stars do because they provide entertainment.

Write a composition of about 200 words stating whether you think football players are paid too much or not. Explain your view. Give specific examples about football and about other kinds of work.

Idea List

_____   _____

_____   _____

_____   _____

_____   _____

_____   _____

_____   _____

▼ **Answers** to Step 2 Practice Exercises are on page 123.

▼ **Extra Practice**. Use Step 2 Review on pages 82–83 for extra help.

C. Application

Look back at the topic you chose in Part C of Step 1 on pages 14 and 15. (You may tear out page 15, if it would be easier to work with that way.)

▼ Make your idea list for that topic.

Idea List

Grouping and Naming

ORGANIZING

A. Instruction

With Step 2 complete, you have assembled the basic ideas you will need to write an essay. Now it is time to organize the ideas into groups. This will make it easier to put the ideas into place—to put them where you need them, when you need them.

Here's the way one student organized her list of ideas into groups. Lynn is working on the writing assignment about "The Effects of Owning a Car." After she had circled the topic and underlined the instructions, she wrote the following list:

The Effects of Owning a Car

impress friends
sense of identity
freedom
won't have to ask parents
    for their car
won't have to ride with others
can have a job
take friends places
go out for rides
cost of gas
cost of insurance
cost of parts
take pride in car
take good care of it
sense of independence
sense of responsibility

How did Lynn divide her list into groups? Lynn had no trouble dividing her list into two groups: a group of good effects and a group of bad effects.

The Effects of Owning a Car

Good Effects
impress friends
sense of identity
freedom
won't have to ask
   parents for their car
won't have to ride
   with others
can have a job
take friends places
go out for rides
take pride in car
take good care of it
sense of independence
sense of responsibility

Bad Effects
cost of gas
cost of insurance
cost of parts

Lynn had more good effects than bad effects on her list. She decided to divide the group of good effects into two groups. Then she would have three groups in all.

Why make three groups? As you will see later, the topic of your composition must have strong support. Each group will become a paragraph that supports your topic. Having three strong paragraphs will insure that you have enough support for your topic. After you make your list and divide it into two groups, divide the bigger of your two groups to make three.

Lynn looked at her list of good effects. She saw that she had written two different kinds of good effects. One had to do with how owning a car would give her new freedom. The other had to do with how owning a car would give her new responsibility.

SUMMARY

Try to make at least three groups from your list of ideas. You can start with two groups, then divide one of them.

Lynn saw that she could make two groups of good effects. She divided her good effects into the following groups:

Freedom
won't have to ask parents for their car
won't have to ride with others
take friends places
go out for rides
sense of independence
visit friends

Responsibility
can have a job
take pride in car
take good care of it

Notice that Lynn used two of her ideas to name her groups. Sometimes your ideas can help you name your groups. Lynn also thought of another effect while she was making these groups. She thought that she could use her car to go visit her friends. Organizing your ideas can often help you come up with additional ones.

But two of Lynn's ideas didn't fit in her groups. She left "impress friends" and "sense of identity" off her lists. Grouping the common ideas on your list can show you ones that might not fit.

Lynn named her groups "bad effects," "good effects—freedom," and "good effects—responsibility." Naming your groups helps you remember what the ideas in each group have in common.

Already you can see how Lynn will write her essay. She will state her topic: owning a car can affect your life in many ways. Her three groups will become the three paragraphs that support her topic in the essay she will write. One paragraph will be about the bad effects of owning a car. Another will be about how owning a car can give you new freedom. Another will be about how owning a car can give you new responsibility. Organizing your ideas this way really makes writing much easier!

SUMMARY

Always ask yourself, "Do all the ideas in each group have something in common? Does the name of each group really tell the common idea of that group?"

B. Practice

1. Read the list that Carl wrote on the topic "My Opinion of Skateboards."

Skateboards

good exercise
chance of injury
problem finding safe
  culverts to do tricks in
tricks can be dangerous
gives kids goals to
  strive for

develop balance
good way to travel
good activity for friends
  to do together
trick contests can be fun
  and challenging
status symbol

First Carl divided his list into two groups: good things about skateboards and problems with skateboards. He had thought of more good things than bad things, so he divided the good things into two groups in order to end up with three groups.

▼ Read the names he gave the groups below.

▼ Look at the list of ideas.

▼ Put the ideas under the names that describe them.

Good Aspects

Health	Self-Concept	Problems
_____	_____	_____
_____	_____	_____
_____	_____	_____
_____	_____	_____
_____	_____	_____
_____	_____	_____

2. Read the writing assignment below. Then read how Jeff grouped the ideas he had put in a list.

In our society today, people may move every few years. By moving often, people can experience different places and climates. They can also meet many new people and make new friends. But some people prefer to stay in one place all their lives and never move far from home. They feel secure in a place they know and like to keep the same friends and neighbors.

Write a composition of about 200 words stating whether you think it is better to stay in one place or to move often and live in different places. Be specific. Give examples to support your view.

▼ Name each group by writing the main idea above each group.

Group A

Name _____

_____

know where every-

   thing is

keep same friends

can have pets

_____

_____

_____

Group B

Name _____

_____

more experiences

new things to see

   and do

new friends

may have new

   climate

_____

Group C

Name _____

_____

change schools

leave friends

learn way around

   new area

feel like a stranger

   at first

pack up everything

might be hard to

   have pets

3. Look back at the writing assignment and the idea list you made on page 22.

> **Topic:** State whether you think football players are paid too much or not.

▼ Divide your list into three groups.

▼ Name your groups.

▼ Write the groups and their names on the lines below.

Name _____   **Name** _____   **Name** _____

_____   _____   _____

_____   _____   _____

_____   _____   _____

_____   _____   _____

_____   _____   _____

_____   _____   _____

_____   _____   _____

_____   _____   _____

_____   _____   _____

_____   _____   _____

> ▼ **Answers** to Step 3 Practice Exercises are on page 124.
>
> ▼ **Extra Practice**. Use Step 3 Review on pages 84–85 for extra help.

C. Application

Look back at the idea list you made in Part C of Step 2 on page 23.

▼ Organize it into three strong groups.

▼ Name each group.

Name _____

_____

_____

_____

_____

Name _____

_____

_____

_____

_____

Name _____

_____

_____

_____

_____

Adding Details and
Putting Groups in Order

ORGANIZING

A. Instruction

You have named and grouped the ideas in your list. Now you are ready to take a good look at each group. How can you improve the groups?

1. Can you think of specific examples to illustrate your ideas? Reread what you have written. Add details.

2. Can you put the details and examples in order? Decide on an order for the details within each group.

3. Can you put the groups in order? Decide on an order for the groups.

Giving specific examples, facts, and details will bring your writing alive for your readers. Sometimes this involves a personal experience—telling about the time car repairs ruined your vacation. Sometimes it involves reporting facts. Which statement is more convincing? *Car insurance costs a lot of money.* **or** *Car insurance costs hundreds of dollars a year.*

It is also important to organize your list of ideas. Organizing your lists will make it easier for you to write your composition. Remember that your ideas will become your composition. Your groups will become the paragraphs that support your topic. Adding more details and examples to your groups will make your paragraphs stronger. Putting the details and the groups in order will make your composition flow well.

One way to order your ideas is to start with the WEAKEST ideas and end with the STRONGEST. Think of great speeches you have heard or read. They usually build up gradually and end with a POW. You can make your paragraphs build to a POW at the end. Put your ideas in order from weakest to strongest.

SUMMARY

Expand and order in three steps:

1. **Add specific details and examples to each of your groups.**

2. **Put the ideas in each group in order.**

3. **Put the groups in order.**

One way to build a paragraph or composition is begin with the WEAKEST ideas and end with the STRONGEST.

Below is one of the three groups that Lynn had developed from her idea list on the effects of owning a car.

Bad Effects
cost of gas
cost of insurance
cost of parts

Lynn knew that specific examples would make her essay more interesting and easier to write. She tried to remember why she had thought of each idea. She remembered the $12 it had cost her to fill up her mom's car. Write "$12 to fill up" beside "cost of gas." She remembered her dad saying that insurance costs hundreds of dollars. Write "Where would I get hundreds of dollars?" beside "cost of insurance." While she was doing this, Lynn thought of another bad effect. She would probably have to get a job to afford a car. Add "have to get a job—less free time" to the list. When she thought about "cost of parts," she remembered her family's last vacation. Their car had broken down in a little town, and they had been stranded for two days. Add "repairs are a pain—stuck for 2 days" to Lynn's list.

Lynn was pleased. She had added specific examples and more ideas to her list. She knew the more specific she made her essay, the more interesting it would be to her readers. She added examples to her other two groups.

Now it was time to put these details and examples in order. Lynn knew that each group would become a paragraph. So she had to decide what to write about first, second, third, and so on.

The Effects of Owning a Car

① *Bad Effects*

2 - cost of gas - $12 to fill up
5 - cost of insurance - where would I
    get hundreds of dollars?
3 - cost of parts
1 - have to get a job - less free time
4 - repairs are a pain - stuck for
    2 days

Lynn knew that a good way to order ideas is to start with the weakest idea and end with the strongest. She thought about the ideas in her "Bad Effects" group. She thought that her weakest idea was "have to get a job." She actually thought it might be exciting to get a job. She wrote a **1** by it. "Cost of gas" was the next least important idea to her. She wrote a **2** by it. She wrote a **3** by "cost of parts" and a **4** by "repairs are a pain." The idea that worried her most was getting the money to pay for insurance. She wrote a **5** beside "cost of insurance." Would you have placed these ideas in the same order? Why or why not?

Now Lynn had her ideas listed from the least important to the most important. She also ordered the ideas in the other two groups. She looked at all three groups. She decided that "Bad Effects" was her weakest group. It wasn't as important to her as the other groups. She would start with it.

Lynn looked at her other two groups. She asked herself which group was stronger. She felt that it was important that a car would give her new responsibility. She thought, however, that the effect a car would have on her personal freedom was more important. She decided to put the "Good Effects— Freedom" group at the end because that was the point she most wanted her readers to remember.

B. Practice

1. Carl is working on a composition about "My Opinion of Skateboards."

   ▼ Read the three groups of ideas he wrote.

   Group A: Good Aspects—Health

   good exercise_____

   develop balance_____

   Group B: Good Aspects—Self-Concept

   good way to travel_____

   good activity for friends to do together_____

   trick contests can be fun and challenging_____

   gives kids goals to strive for_____

   status symbol_____

   Group C: Problems

   chance of injury_____

   problem finding safe culverts to do tricks in_____

   _____

   tricks can be dangerous_____

   ▼ Add more details or examples to the groups if you can think of any.

   ▼ Now think about how the details in each group should be put in order. You can make notes by writing small numerals beside the details.

   ▼ Think about which group of ideas is the weakest argument and which group is the strongest argument. You can make notes by writing small numerals beside the group names.

4

▼ Write the groups and the ideas in order below.

Group 1 _____

_____

_____

_____

_____

_____

_____

Group 2 _____

_____

_____

_____

_____

_____

_____

Group 3 _____

_____

_____

_____

_____

_____

_____

▼ **Answers** to Step 4 Practice Exercises are on page 125.

▼ **Extra Practice**. Use Step 4 Review on pages 86–87 for extra help.

C. Application

You have already completed three steps of the writing of your composition. First, you came to understand your topic. Second, you listed your ideas about the topic. Third, you grouped the ideas to make three specific paragraphs to support your topic. Now you are ready to expand and order your lists.

▼ Look back at your lists on page 31. Can you think of any more details or examples to add?

▼ When you are satisfied that you have enough details, you can put them in order within each group. Put your weakest ideas first. Put your strongest ideas last. Rely on your own good sense. Trust yourself. Don't try to guess what your teacher or someone else would think is strong or weak. If you do, your paper will seem phony.

▼ Decide the order of your three groups: weakest to strongest.

▼ Take some time to think about your decision. Give your reasons for your decision in your own words. By writing out your thoughts, you'll think them through more clearly.

Reasons _____

_____

_____

_____

_____

_____

_____

_____

4

▼ Now write your groups and ideas in order on the lines below.

Group 1 _____

_____

_____

_____

_____

_____

Group 2 _____

_____

_____

_____

_____

_____

_____

Group 3 _____

_____

_____

_____

_____

_____

_____

Writing the Introductory Paragraph

WRITING

A. Instruction

Now your groups are in the best order possible. They are as full of strong, specific supporting details as you can make them. What do you do next? Write!

The first paragraph will introduce your readers to your composition. It is called the **introductory paragraph**. It tells your readers two important things. It states the topic clearly. Then it tells how you plan to approach your topic. In other words, it gives your readers a preview of your whole composition.

The sentence that states your topic is called your **topic sentence**. It is usually the first sentence of your introductory paragraph. The topic sentence gives the general subject that you will discuss in your essay.

Lynn read the topic in the assignment she has been working on: "Describe how owning a car might affect your life." She based her topic sentence on the topic given in the assignment. Look at the topic sentence she wrote.

Owning a car would affect my life in many ways, both good and bad.

SUMMARY

A good introductory paragraph does two things:

1. It states the topic.
2. It tells your reader how you will approach the topic.

Notice that it is a more interesting sentence because Lynn didn't simply restate the topic. She changed "might" to "would." She also put the words "in many ways" and "both good and bad" in her topic sentence.

You can almost always create your topic sentence by rewriting the topic. Study these examples. Notice that the topic sentence is forceful and direct. Extra words or a phrase of your own can help.

Topic: Discuss the advantages and disadvantages of owning a pet.

Topic Sentence: Before choosing a pet for yourself, it is important to understand the advantages and disadvantages of owning a pet.

Topic: State whether you think life is better in the city or the country.

Topic Sentence: Although many people live in the city and enjoy it greatly, I feel that life in the country is really much better.

Sometimes the writing assignment topic may be in the form of a question. You can write a good topic sentence by changing the question to a statement. Study the examples below. Notice that each topic sentence is based on the question in the assignment.

Topic: What are the advantages and disadvantages of being famous?

Topic Sentence: Being famous would have its advantages, but there would be certain disadvantages also.

Topic: Why is it important for people to vote in local elections?

Topic Sentence: Although it may be hard to find the time, it is important for people to vote in local elections.

SUMMARY

Write the topic sentence from the topic.

Now what does Lynn need to write to complete her introductory paragraph? She needs to write **preview sentences**. Preview sentences usually follow the topic sentence. They give readers an idea of what to expect in the whole composition.

How do you know what to write as preview sentences for an introductory paragraph? Think back to Steps 3 and 4. In Step 3, you grouped and named your ideas. In Step 4, you ordered your ideas and your groups. You can use the names of your groups to write your preview sentences.

Look at the names Lynn gave her groups. Then look at the preview sentences Lynn added to her topic sentence to make her introductory paragraph.

Groups: Bad Effects (cost)
Good Effects - Responsibility
Good Effects - Freedom

Owning a car would affect my life in many ways, both good and bad. Owning a car would create new expenses and problems for me. But a car would also give me new responsibility and freedom.

Do you see how Lynn used the names of her groups to write her preview sentences? If you have grouped and organized your ideas well, you can easily create the preview sentences for your introductory paragraph.

B. Practice

1. Below is a topic from a writing assignment.

   ▼ Read the topic.
   ▼ Read the introductory paragraph.
   ▼ Copy the introductory paragraph on the lines provided.
   ▼ Underline the topic sentence with two lines.

   Topic: Why is regular exercise good for your health?

   ### Introductory Paragraph

   Regular exercise is good for your general health. This paper will discuss three important benefits of regular exercise: better muscle tone, a stronger heart, and more stamina.

   ### Introductory Paragraph

   _____

   _____

   _____

   _____

   _____

   _____

   _____

   _____

   _____

2. Below is a topic from another writing assignment.

▼ Read the topic.
▼ Read the introductory paragraph.
▼ Copy the introductory paragraph on the lines provided.
▼ Underline the preview sentences with one line.

Topic: Explain your own opinion of skateboards.

Introductory Paragraph

Many people feel that skateboards are dangerous, but I feel that skateboards provide many good things. Skateboards can cause problems if they are used carelessly. But if you use skateboards wisely, they can help your health and your self-concept.

Introductory Paragraph

_____

_____

_____

_____

_____

_____

_____

_____

_____

3. Look at the following topic and introductory paragraph. The introductory paragraph needs help. Read it and look for problems.

> **Topic:** What are the advantages of shopping at a large supermarket that sells more than just food?

Convenience	**Savings**
just one trip	save gas
big choice	things on sale
all in the same place	can use coupons

Introductory Paragraph

What are the advantages of shopping at a large supermarket? This is a question that many people ask. This paper is going to answer this question because so many people have asked it. There must be reasons or why would we shop there? I prefer to shop there myself.

Find What Is Wrong

a. What is the topic sentence? _____

_____

b. Is it a forceful statement of the writer's position? _____

c. What are the preview sentences? _____

_____

_____

_____

_____

_____

d. Do the preview sentences reflect the group names? _____

e. Do the preview sentences tell how the writer will approach the topic? _____

f. Are there extra sentences that mislead or confuse you? _____

▼ Reread the topic. Write a better topic sentence.

_____

_____

_____

▼ Use the names of the groups to write preview sentences.

_____

_____

_____

_____

_____

_____

_____

_____

_____

_____

Analyze Your Paragraph

▼ Does your topic sentence state your position clearly? _____

▼ Do your preview sentences tell how you will approach the topic? _____

▼ Is your paragraph interesting and direct? _____

4. Now you are ready to write on your own.

▼ Read the topic and look at the organized groups.

▼ Write an introductory paragraph for the topic below. You can use the groups shown or create your own groups to work from.

Topic: State whether you think it is better to stay in one place or to move often and live different places.

Stay in One Place Advantages	Move Advantages	Move Disadvantages
know where everything is	more experiences	change schools
keep same friends	new things to see and do	leave friends
can have pets	new friends	learn way around new area
	may have new climate	feel like a stranger at first
		pack up everything
		might be hard to have pets

Your Introductory Paragraph

_____

_____

_____

_____

_____

_____

5. Write an introductory paragraph for the topic below. Use the groups you made on page 30.

▼ Write the topic sentence from the topic.

▼ Write the preview sentences from the names of your groups.

> **Topic:** State whether you think football players are paid too much or not.

_____

_____

_____

_____

_____

_____

_____

_____

_____

_____

_____

_____

▼ **Answers** to Step 5 Practice Exercises are on page 126.

▼ **Extra Practice.** Use Step 5 Review on pages 88–89 for extra help.

C. Application

You are now ready to begin writing the first paragraph of your composition. Your introductory paragraph will state your topic and tell your readers how you will approach the topic.

▼ Look back at the topic you chose to write about on page 15.

▼ Write the topic on the lines below.

Topic _____

_____

_____

▼ Write the introductory paragraph for your composition.

▼ Use the topic to write your topic sentence.

▼ Study the groups you expanded and organized in Step 4 on page 39.

▼ Use these groups—especially their names—to write preview sentences for your introductory paragraph.

Your Introductory Paragraph

_____

_____

_____

_____

_____

_____

_____

Writing the Body
of Your Paper

WRITING

A. Instruction

Now that you have written an introduction, you are ready to begin the main part of your composition, the **body**. But first, let's review where you are in the POWER plan for writing a composition.

1. You have read the writing assignment. You have found the topic. You have also understood the importance of the background and the instructions.

2. You have listed your ideas.

3. You have divided your list into three groups.

4. You have expanded and ordered each group.

5. You have written an introduction with a topic sentence and preview sentences that show how your composition will develop.

It is time to write the **body** of your paper, the main part of the composition. You will use your groups to build the body of your paper. You will turn each group into a paragraph, using the details in each group to write the sentences you need.

Remember how you changed the topic in the writing assignment into the topic sentence for your introductory paragraph? You also used the names of your groups as the preview sentences in your introductory paragraph. Now you will use each group name to write a topic sentence for each paragraph of the body. You will use the details listed under each group name to write the sentences in each paragraph. You can add explanations and examples as needed.

SUMMARY

The name of each group becomes the topic sentence of each paragraph.

The ideas listed under each group name become the sentences for each paragraph.

Lynn wrote her introductory paragraph in Step 5. The introductory paragraph she wrote is given below.

Owning a car would affect my life in many ways, both good and bad. Owning a car would create new expenses and problems for me. But a car would also give me new responsibility and freedom.

Now let's see how she builds the body of her paper. She takes her first group as a starting point. Lynn felt that her group about the bad effects of owning a car was the weakest, so she begins with that group. Her group name becomes the basis for the topic sentence.

Group Name: Bad Effects

Lynn's Topic Sentence:

Although I would love to own a car, I realize that a car would create expenses and problems for me.

Next, Lynn uses the ideas under the group name to write the sentences for her first paragraph. Look at the ideas Lynn listed. See how she uses these ideas to make sentences for her paragraph. Notice that sometimes she adds or leaves out ideas to make her paragraph clear and strong.

Bad Effects

have to get a job—less free time
cost of gas—$12 to fill up
cost of parts
repairs are a pain—stuck for 2 days
cost of insurance—Where would I get hundreds of dollars?

> Although I would love to own a car, I realize that a car would create expenses and problems for me. To afford a car, I would need to get a job. I don't think I'd mind working, but I might not have as much time to spend with my friends. If I had a car, I would have to pay for gas, parts, and insurance. This could really add up. When I filled up my mom's car, it cost $12. Car repairs can be very expensive, not to mention being a pain. On our last vacation, my family was stranded in a tiny town for two days because of car repairs. I worry most about insurance, though. Car insurance costs hundreds of dollars every year. I would have to save my money to pay for insurance.

Notice how closely Lynn follows the organization she had worked on earlier. Notice that she adds some things, leaves out other things, and combines some things into stronger statements. When she is finished, she has written a strong paragraph for the body of her composition.

B. Practice

1. You just read how Lynn took her first expanded group and wrote the sentences for the first paragraph in the body of her composition.

   ▼ Take Lynn's second expanded group, "Good Effects—Responsibility," and write the second paragraph of the body of her composition. The first two sentences have been done for you.

   ▼ You may rearrange the order of the ideas. You may rewrite the first two sentences and replace them with your own. You may leave out ideas that do not work for you. You may add ideas you feel help the meaning. The point is to write the best, clearest paragraph you can.

   Good Effects—Responsibility

   take pride in car
   take good care of it—wash it, learn to work on it
   can have a job

   Owning a car would mean that I would have more

   responsibility. I could take pride in owning my very own car.

   _____

   _____

   _____

   _____

   _____

   _____

   _____

   _____

   _____

2. Now read Lynn's third group, "Good Effects—Freedom."

▼ Write the third paragraph of the body of her composition.

▼ Remember to write the topic sentence from the name of the group.

▼ You may rearrange the order of the ideas. You may leave out ideas that do not work for you. You may add ideas you feel help the meaning. The point is to write the best, clearest paragraph you can.

Good Effects—Freedom

go out for rides
visit friends
take friends places—to school, shopping
won't have to ride with others
won't have to ask parents for their car
sense of independence

_____

_____

_____

_____

_____

_____

_____

_____

_____

▼ **Answers** to Step 6 Practice Exercises are on page 127.

▼ **Extra Practice**. Use Step 6 Review on pages 90–91 for extra help.

C. Application

You wrote your introductory paragraph in Step 5 on page 50. Now you are ready to write the body of your composition.

▼ Reread your introduction on page 50.

▼ Reread your expanded groups on page 39.

▼ Use your expanded groups to write the paragraphs of the body of your composition.

▼ Use the name of each group to write the topic sentence of each paragraph.

▼ Use the ideas listed under each group name to write the sentences for each paragraph.

Paragraph 1

_____

_____

_____

_____

_____

_____

_____

_____

_____

_____

_____

Paragraph 2

_____

_____

_____

_____

_____

_____

_____

_____

_____

Paragraph 3

_____

_____

_____

_____

_____

_____

_____

_____

_____

_____

Writing the Concluding Paragraph

WRITING

A. Instruction

The last paragraph of your composition is called the **concluding paragraph**. In a way, it has the same purpose as the introductory paragraph, only in reverse. It tells what you have written. It restates your topic and reviews your supporting ideas. A good concluding paragraph ties everything together and convinces the reader that you have made your point.

In writing the concluding paragraph, you might be tempted simply to repeat the introductory paragraph in different words. But repeating what you have already said is boring for the writer and for the reader as well. When you have succeeded in writing a good composition, why spoil it with a last paragraph that makes your readers yawn? Keep your composition interesting right up to the end. Use the last paragraph to sum up your main ideas, give some final advice, or express your opinions. Or propose a solution to the problems you have mentioned. Whatever you choose, make your concluding paragraph strong!

Read the composition on the following pages. In it, Lynn discusses how owning a car might affect her life. Her introductory paragraph states the topic clearly and tells the reader how she will approach the topic. The next three paragraphs make up the body of her composition. She used the name of each of her groups to write the topic sentence of each body paragraph. (The topic sentence of each body paragraph is underlined.) She used the ideas under each group name to write the sentences for each of these paragraphs.

Pay particular attention to her concluding paragraph. See how she uses it to tie up her composition. She refers back to the points in the introductory paragraph and provides a strong, clear ending to her composition.

SUMMARY

A concluding paragraph should do three things:

1. tie up your composition
2. relate to the points in the introductory paragraph
3. provide a strong, clear ending to your composition

Don't simply restate the points made in your introductory paragraph. Use opinions or solutions to keep your reader's interest.

The Effects of Owning a Car

Introduction

Owning a car would affect my life in many ways, both good and bad. Owning a car would create new expenses and problems for me. But a car would also give me new responsibility and freedom.

Body Paragraph 1

Although I would love to own a car, I realize that a car would create expenses and problems for me. To afford a car, I would need to get a job. I don't think I'd mind working, but I might not have as much time to spend with my friends. If I had a car, I would have to pay for gas, parts, and insurance. Gas could really add up. When I filled up my mom's car, it cost $12. Car repairs can be very expensive, not to mention being a pain. On our last vacation, my family was stranded in a tiny town for two days because of car repairs. I worry most about insurance, though. Car insurance costs hundreds of dollars every year. I would have to save my money to pay for insurance.

Body Paragraph 2

Owning a car would mean that I would have more responsibility. I could take pride in owning my very own car. I would take good care of it. I would wash my car often, and maybe even learn to work on it. If I had a car, I could get a job. I would have transportation to and from work. Then I would learn the responsibility of keeping a job and also of spending my money wisely.

Body Paragraph 3

The best effect of owning a car would be the freedom it would give me. I could do so many things that I can't do now. I could go out for rides in the country. I could visit my friends and take them places. I could give my best friend a ride to school, and we could go shopping on our own. I wouldn't have to ask other people for rides or ask my parents if I could borrow their car. Having a car of my own would give me a wonderful feeling of freedom and independence.

Conclusion

How would owning a car affect my life? It would give me many things that I do not have now: expenses, problems, responsibilities, and freedom. How would I handle the good effects and the bad effects of owning a car? I would love the good effects and learn to live with the bad effects. Owning a car *would be a turning point in my life. It would be another step to becoming an adult.*

Look closely at Lynn's first and last paragraphs. Does she mention in her concluding paragraph the points she talked about in her introductory paragraph?

Introduction

1. Owning a car has good effects and bad effects.

2. Owning a car creates new expenses and problems.

3. A car can provide a sense of responsibility and freedom.

Conclusion

1. How would I handle the good effects and bad effects?

2. Owning a car would make many changes in my life.

3. Owning a car would be a turning point in my life.

You can see that Lynn's concluding paragraph does indeed relate to the points brought up in her introductory paragraph. She uses the topic of her composition to organize two overall questions. These questions, "How would owning a car affect my life?" and "How would I handle the good effects and the bad effects of owning a car?" state the topic in a more interesting way. Lynn answers the questions with several general statements that sum up the main ideas of her paper. She also introduces the new, persuasive idea that having a car would be a step toward adulthood. Lynn's concluding paragraph is interesting, clear, and strong.

B. Practice

1. In the following composition, the concluding paragraph needs help. The introductory paragraph and body are fine, but the conclusion has gone off the topic.

▼ Read the topic and the composition.

> **Topic**: Explain your own opinion of skateboards.

Many people feel that skateboards are dangerous, but I feel that skateboards provide many good things. Skateboards can cause problems if they are used carelessly. But if you use skateboards wisely, they can improve your health and your self-concept.

Skateboarding does have some problems. Kids sometimes can't find safe culverts to do tricks in, so they skateboard in dangerous places. Some kids are daredevils and attempt dangerous tricks. If this happens, then there is a chance of injury. Some skateboarders get scrapes, sprained ankles, and even broken bones. But if you are not reckless, skateboarding is no more dangerous than any other sport.

Skateboarding can be very good for your health. It is good exercise. It makes your heart pump faster and your leg muscles stronger. Skateboarding helps develop your balance and coordination.

Riding a skateboard can improve the way you feel about yourself. It is a good activity for friends to do together because it is something you can share. A skateboard can be a status symbol. It can make you feel more like a part of the group. Tricks can be fun and challenging. I think the best effect of skateboarding is that it gives you goals to strive for. If you become skillful on a skateboard, you can use that confidence and discipline to become skillful in other areas.

Conclusion

Skateboarding is one of my favorite activities. I do it all the time with my friends. In fact, my mom says skateboarding is all I ever do. She wishes I'd spend that much time doing my homework. So do my teachers. But take it from me, skateboarding is cool!

▼ Write a better concluding paragraph.

_____

_____

_____

_____

_____

_____

_____

_____

_____

_____

_____

_____

_____

_____

_____

_____

_____

2. The composition below needs a concluding paragraph.

▼ Read the topic.

> **Topic:** State whether you think it is better to stay in one place or to move often and live different places.

▼ Read the groups and note the order.

Group 1 Move Advantages	Group 2 Move Disadvantages	Group 3 Stay in One Place Advantages

more experiences
may have new
  climate
new friends
new things to see
  and do
	pack up everything
	leave friends
	change schools
	feel like a stranger
	  at first
	learn way around
	  new area
	might be hard to
	  have pets
		know where
		  everything is
		can have pets
		keep same friends

▼ Read the introductory paragraph and body.

Although there are advantages and disadvantages to both, I prefer being settled in one place to moving often. Moving often causes many exciting changes, but it also creates many difficulties. Living in one place provides many benefits.

Moving often would have some advantages. You would have many new, exciting experiences. You might experience a completely different climate and type of country. You would meet new people and probably make new friends. There would be many new things to see and do.

On the other hand, moving often would also have many disadvantages. You would have to pack up everything you owned and move. You would have to leave all your friends and change schools. You might feel like a stranger and be lonely at first. It would take some time to learn your way around the new area. If you moved often, it would probably be difficult to keep pets.

Staying in one place allows you to have much stability in your life. You would know where everything is and would get to know the people in your community. If you needed help, you could ask one of your friends or neighbors. If you wanted, you could have pets. The best effect would be that you could keep the same friends for as long as you wanted.

▼ Write a concluding paragraph.

_____

_____

_____

_____

_____

_____

_____

_____

_____

_____

▼ **Answers** to Step 7 Practice Exercises are on page 127.

▼ **Extra Practice**. Use Step 7 Review on pages 92–93 for extra help.

C. Application

You wrote your introductory paragraph in Step 5 on page 50. You wrote the body of your composition in Step 6 on pages 57-58.

▼ Reread the paragraphs of your composition you have already written.

▼ Write the concluding paragraph for your composition. Remember to link your introductory and concluding paragraphs.

_____

_____

_____

_____

_____

_____

_____

_____

_____

_____

_____

_____

_____

_____

Improving Your Composition

EVALUATING & REVISING

A. Instruction

The concluding paragraph is the last paragraph in your composition. But finishing that paragraph doesn't mean the job is done. There's still one step left. You must **evaluate** and **revise** your composition.

Evaluate first. Read over your composition. Focus on your introductory paragraph. What did you say you were going to write about? When you read the rest of the composition, does it talk about *only* what you said it would talk about? If yes, then you have stuck to the topic. If no, then you must revise your composition by taking out parts that are off the topic.

Next, ask yourself if you have provided enough support for your topic. Think like a lawyer at this point. Your whole composition must convince your readers—the jury—that what you said in your introductory paragraph is true or makes sense. Will your composition convince your readers? Are there enough examples and details to make a good case? If not, this is your last chance to strengthen your argument. Add examples and details where your composition needs them.

When you evaluate, you decide what to do to improve your composition. When you revise, you do what you have decided. Leave out sentences and ideas that are off the topic. Add examples and details for a stronger composition. You also need to correct any errors you might find. You need to check for errors in sentence structure, capitalization, punctuation, and spelling. Look at the Writer's Handbook on pages 112 to 122 for examples of the kinds of errors to look for and correct.

Now let's look at how Lynn evaluated and revised her composition about the effects of owning a car.

Lynn reread her composition on pages 61 through 63 and reviewed it carefully. She asked herself if she had stayed on the topic. She asked herself if she had provided enough support for her topic. She felt that she had.

SUMMARY

When you evaluate, ask yourself three questions:

1. Did I stick to the topic?

2. Did I provide enough support for my topic?

3. How can I improve my composition?

Then Lynn asked herself how she could improve her composition. She noticed that in her paragraph about the bad effects of owning a car, she mentioned having a job. She also mentioned having a job in her paragraph about good effects—responsibility. She thought that her composition would be stronger if she mentioned having a job in only one place. She decided to take it out of the bad effects paragraph since she really did want to get a job. So she deleted the sentences about having a job from her bad effects paragraph and reworded the last sentence. Read her revised paragraph:

> Although I would love to own a car, I realize that a car would create expenses and problems for me. If I had a car, I would have to pay for gas, parts, and insurance. Gas could really add up. When I filled up my mom's car, it cost $12. Car repairs can be very expensive, not to mention being a pain. On our last vacation, my family was stranded in a tiny town for two days because of car repairs. I worry most about insurance, though. Car insurance costs hundreds of dollars every year. I would have to save my money to pay for insurance.

She noticed that the revision made the paragraph about the same length as the other two paragraphs in the body. She was glad that now her composition was more balanced and did not have contradictory statements.

You have gone through all eight writing steps with Lynn. You know that she developed a strong idea list and stayed on topic throughout her composition. When she evaluated her composition, she found that she needed to revise only a small part of it.

Now let's look at Pat's composition. Unlike Lynn, Pat did not start with a strong idea list, so she had trouble providing enough support for her topic. She also went off the topic at one point.

Let's see how Pat evaluated and revised her composition.

Topic: State whether you think it is better to stay in one place or to move often and live different places.

Idea List

exciting
more experiences
new things to see and do
new countryside

Many people live in one place their entire lives and enjoy it, but I prefer experiencing different places. Living in one place provides security, but there are many disadvantages to this lifestyle. Living in new places is exciting and educational.

Moving to a different city or town is an adventure. Everything will be unfamiliar to you. You will have new experiences. You will have different things to see and do. Maybe you will be near mountains or the ocean. You could learn to ski or surf. Moving can give you opportunities you didn't have before. But remember, long-distance phone calls are expensive. Best of all, you will be able to meet a variety of people and make many new friends.

So be brave! Find a place you think you'd like, then pack up and move. You'll have many more exciting experiences than people who stay in one place all their lives.

Pat reread her composition and carefully reviewed her introductory paragraph. What did she say she would talk about in her composition? She said she preferred living in different places. She said living in one place provided security but many disadvantages.

Pat asked herself if there was any place in her composition where she went off topic. She found a sentence in her second paragraph that didn't seem to fit. She took out "But remember, long-distance phone calls are expensive." She thought all her other sentences were on topic.

Then Pat looked at her idea list. She had only one list—the advantages of moving. She also had only one paragraph in the body of her paper. She thought her essay would be more convincing if she added more ideas to support her topic.

In her introductory paragraph she had said, "Living in one place provides security, but there are many disadvantages to this lifestyle." She realized she could make two other lists from these ideas. She could write about the advantages of living in one place and the disadvantages of living in one place. She decided to write two new lists.

Revised Idea List

Living in One Place Advantages	Living in One Place Disadvantages
security of a routine people would help you can get checks cashed	can't escape past everyone knows everything about you fewer opportunities boring

Pat used her new ideas to write two new paragraphs for the body of her paper. Read her revised essay.

Many people live in one place their entire lives and enjoy it, but I prefer experiencing different places. Living in one place provides security, but there are many disadvantages to this lifestyle. Living in new places is exciting and educational.

Living in one place for a long time does have some advantages. You know where everything is and have the security of a routine. If you need help, you can ask a friend or neighbor. It is easy to cash checks and conduct other business because everyone knows you.

For me these advantages are overshadowed by the disadvantages of staying in one place. Especially in a small town, you can't escape your past. Everyone knows everything about you. Often educational and job opportunities are limited. The biggest disadvantage is that everything stays the same—to me that means boredom!

Moving to a different city or town is an adventure. Everything will be unfamiliar to you. You will have new experiences. You will have different things to see and do. Maybe you will be near mountains or the ocean. You could learn to ski or surf. Moving can give you opportunities you didn't have before. Best of all, you will be able to meet a variety of people and make many new friends.

So be brave! Find a place you think you'd like, then pack up and move. You'll have many more exciting experiences than people who stay in one place all their lives.

Did you notice the details Pat added? The body now has three paragraphs instead of one. By rechecking her topic and evaluating her idea list, Pat was able to add two more paragraphs to support her topic. These changes made her composition stronger and more convincing.

You can see the value of evaluating and revising your composition. After you have written your composition, read it and analyze it. A first draft will probably not be perfect, but you can fix it when you revise. You can add punctuation where it is needed. You can add letters, words, and phrases by writing them in. You can delete something you don't want by crossing it out. You can cross out misspelled words and write in the correct spelling. You can use circles and arrows to show where words should be moved. Then you can rewrite your composition perfectly!

B. Practice

Read Jim's composition.

> **Topic:** Discuss the advantages and disadvantages of owning an automobile.

Idea List

Advantages

easy transportation
more convenient than bus
fun—music, vacations
carry things

Disadvantages

driver's license test
expenses
  insurance
  upkeep and gas
  repairs

Millions of Americans drive automobiles every day. Sometimes they like owning their cars. Other times they don't. This paper will discuss the advantages and disadvantages of owning an automobile. I own a car and so does my brother. We like to race at the local race track in amateur contests.

There are several important advantages to owning an automobile. A car provides easy transportation right from your house. You don't have to worry about bus routes or waiting for buses. Also, you can have a sound system in your car to listen to music. One great group is Van Halen. I have three of their tapes. Driving along with the windows open and good music playing makes me feel good. Another advantage to having a car is you can carry more packages or groceries than you can carry on a bus.

While owning a car has advantages, it also has disadvantages. You have to get a driver's license. There is a test for this, and some people have to take it more than once to pass. Once you have a license you need car insurance, which costs money. The upkeep and gas for your car costs money, too. Sometimes you have to leave your car for repairs. This costs time and money.

Even though owning a car can cost time and money, the advantages of owning a car outweigh these disadvantages. For convenience, fun, and carrying capacity, an automobile is a must for any adult. Bus riding is okay. My brother and I rode the bus everywhere before we got our cars.

1. Evaluate Jim's composition. Does it stick to the topic? _____

   If not, where did he go wrong? _____

   _____

   Does every sentence support the topic? _____

2. Now revise Jim's composition. Make revisions right on his composition. Write the new parts on the lines below.

   _____

   _____

   _____

   _____

   _____

   _____

▼ **Answers** to Step 8 Practice Exercises are on page 128.

▼ **Extra Practice**. Use Step 8 Review on pages 94–95 for extra help.

C. Application

Reread the composition that you completed in Step 7. You will find your introductory paragraph on page 50, your body on pages 57–58, and your conclusion on page 68. You will need to put all the parts together.

▼ Evaluate your composition. Ask yourself these questions:

Did I stick to the topic?
Did I provide enough support for my topic?
How can I improve my composition?

▼ Revise your composition and rewrite it in your neatest handwriting.

_____

_____

_____

_____

_____

_____

_____

_____

_____

_____

_____

_____

_____

_____

_____

_____

_____

_____

_____

_____

_____

_____

_____

_____

_____

_____

_____

_____

_____

_____

_____

_____

_____

Congratulations!
You have now completed your composition!

Review

STEP 1 Review
Reading the Assignment

Summary

▼ Always look for three things when you read a writing assignment:

1. the topic
2. the background
3. the instructions

Extra Practice (Help)

Read this writing assignment.

Everyone dreams of winning a million dollars. We think all our problems would be solved if we won that much money. But winning a million dollars could also cause problems.

Write a composition of about 200 words. Discuss the good effects and the bad effects of winning a million dollars. Be sure to include specific examples to support your points.

Ted read the writing assignment and wrote this:

Topic __What I would do if I won a million dollars__

Instructions __make your paper 200 words__

Did Ted pick the right topic? Ted said that the assignment asks him to write about what he would do if he won a million dollars. This is not the topic. The topic is "discuss the good effects and the bad effects of winning a million dollars." No matter how good a composition Ted writes, it will not count. Ted did not choose the right topic.

What should Ted have done? He should have circled the topic in the writing assignment just as you did in Step 1. If Ted had circled the topic, he would have seen it very clearly.

HINT: When you look for the topic, look for a sentence that says something like "Write about . . ." or "In 200 words, discuss . . .". The topic is usually in that sentence.

Did Ted write all of the instructions? He wrote "make your paper 200 words" but left out "be sure to include specific examples to support your points." It's useful to know that the words *specific examples* often appear in the instructions. Specific examples are examples that support, clearly and directly, the points you are trying to make.

HINT: If you do not understand a word in the writing assignment, try to guess its meaning. A writing assignment is written so that the background can help you to get the idea. Try to figure out the meaning of any word you do not know by fitting it to the meaning of the writing assignment as a whole.

STEP 2 Review
Listing Your Ideas

Summary

▼ When listing your ideas, remember: READ
$\downarrow$
THINK
$\downarrow$
WRITE

Repeat these steps as often as you need to.

▼ The longer your list of ideas, the stronger your composition will be.

▼ When you've listed as many ideas as you can, rest a bit. Then look at your list. Does it have enough strong ideas to work with?

Extra Practice (Help)

An idea list is an important tool. You will want yours to be the best it can be. Read the idea lists made by two students, Ted and Cathy. Compare their lists. Ask yourself these questions:

1. How long are their lists?

2. How strong are their lists?

3. Is every idea about the topic?

4. Are there any other ideas they could add?

Everyone dreams of winning a million dollars. We think all our problems would be solved if we won that much money. But winning a million dollars could also cause problems.

Write a composition of about 200 words. (Discuss the good) (effects and the bad effects of winning a million dollars.) Be sure to include specific examples to support your points.

Ted's List

buy a sports car
buy land
buy gold
buy expensive clothes
buy VCR
buy compact disc player

Cathy's List

pay off debts
quit job
travel
make investments
people ask for money
charities want money
buy more lottery tickets
unsure of people's reasons
   for wanting to be friends
news reporters bothering you
car repairs are expensive
taxes would take most of it
sounds better than actually is
money can't buy happiness

You will notice that Ted's list is short and includes only what he will buy. He needs to expand his list to include more effects, both good and bad, of winning a million dollars.

Cathy's list is long and fairly strong. The idea "car repairs are expensive" may not be right on the topic, though.

STEP 3 Review
Grouping and Naming

Summary

▼ Try to make at least three groups from your list of ideas. You can start with two groups, then divide one of them.

▼ Always ask yourself, "Do all the ideas in each group have something in common? Does the name of each group really tell the common idea of that group?"

Extra Practice (Help)

Most writing exercises have no right or wrong answers. There are, however, better or worse ways of doing each writing step. By looking at different ways of listing and grouping, you can see the better ways. Then you can look at your own groups and think about what you might change to make them better.

Remember the advice in Step 2. The longer your list is, the stronger your composition will be. It's much easier to make three strong groups if you have a long list of good ideas.

Look at the groups that Ted and Cathy created from their lists. Compare their lists and groups.

Cathy's Groups

Bad Effects—Personal	Bad Effects—From Outside World	Good Effects
money can't buy happiness	sounds better than it actually is	pay off debts
unsure of people's reasons for wanting to be friends	taxes would take most of it	quit job
	charities want money	travel
	people ask for money	make investments
	news reporters bothering you	buy more lottery tickets

Ted's Groups

Things I Could Buy	How It Would Affect Me and Others
sports car	impress friends with stuff
land	use it to make more money
gold	fight about it with parents
expensive clothes	miserable if I ran out of money
VCR	become lazy and a snob
compact disc player	friends might be jealous
nice things for my family and friends	unsure of why others want to be friends
	people would ask for money
	difficult decisions

Cathy first divided her list into good effects and bad effects. When she looked at her list of bad effects, she saw that it easily divided into two other groups—how she thought and felt (personal) and effects from the outside world. She wrote down her lists and named them. Now she has three good lists to work with.

Ted started out with only a list of things he would buy. Then he thought about how his life would change if he won a million dollars. How would it affect him? How would it affect his family and friends? He wrote down all his new ideas. He even thought of a new idea to add to his first list.

Ted had two good groups, but he decided to divide "How It Might Affect Me and Others" into two groups. He divided it into "How It Would Affect Me" and "How It Would Affect Others." While he was making these lists, he noticed that many of the effects he listed were negative ones. Winning a million dollars would certainly make his life more complicated. This kind of "deciding what you think" often happens while you are grouping. Now Ted has plenty of ideas for his paper.

STEP 4 Review
Expanding and Ordering

Summary

▼ Expand and order in three steps:

   1. Add specific details and examples to each of your groups.

   2. Put the ideas in each group in order.

   3. Put the groups in order.

▼ One way to build a paragraph or composition is to begin with the WEAKEST ideas and end with the STRONGEST.

Extra Practice (Help)

Cathy has three good lists. Now she needs to think of specific examples that will clearly illustrate her ideas. She begins with her list of good effects. Beside each item she writes what comes to her mind.

Good Effects

pay off debts—Pay back $10 to my brother, so he'll quit bugging m
quit job—No more low-paying, boring job at XYZ Insurance
               Company! Yuck! I hate filing papers! Freedom!
travel—Hawaii, Alps, Australia, Hollywood!!! Learn to ski!
make investments—Hire a stockbroker. Make another million.
buy more lottery tickets—Lots of them! After all, it worked once!

Now the reader will get a better picture of Cathy's life and how the million dollars will affect her. It is more interesting to read about specific situations than general ones. Cathy writes notes beside her other two lists.

Cathy has completed the first part of Step 4. She has added specific details and examples to her groups. Now she needs to put the ideas in each group in order. She wants to organize each group from the weakest idea to the strongest. She puts a **1** by the idea that is least important to her, a **2** by the next least important idea, and so on. She puts the highest number beside the strongest idea.

Here is the way Cathy orders the ideas in her good effects group.

1–pay off debts
3–quit job
4–travel
5–make investments
2–buy more lottery tickets

"Pay off debts" is the least important idea to her. After all, she only owes her brother $10! She writes a **1** beside that idea. "Buy more lottery tickets" seems like the next least important idea. She writes a **2** beside it. Quitting her job will be a great effect of winning the money. She writes a **3** beside that idea. Even better than not having to work will be the freedom to travel. She writes a **4** beside "travel." Cathy chooses "make investments" as her most important idea. She writes a **5** next to this idea.

Now Cathy looks at her other two groups, "Bad Effects—Personal" and "Bad Effects—From Outside World." She puts the ideas in order according to how important they are to her.

The final part of Step 4 is to put the groups in order. Cathy decides that "Good Effects" is her weakest group, so she puts it first. "Bad Effects— From Outside World" is important. She puts it second. "Bad Effects—Personal" is the most important group to her, so she places it at the end, where it will have the most influence on her readers.

STEP 5 Review
Writing the Introduction

Summary

▼ A good introductory paragraph does two things:

   1. It states the topic.

   2. It tells your reader how you will approach the topic.

▼ Write the topic sentence from the topic.

▼ Write the preview sentences from the names of your groups.

Extra Practice (Help)

Below are the introductory paragraphs Cathy and Ted wrote for their compositions on the good effects and the bad effects of winning a million dollars. Read the paragraphs. Then judge how effective each introductory paragraph is by answering the questions.

Cathy's Introductory Paragraph

I would love to win a million dollars! Think of all the great things I could do—quit my job, pay off my debts, then travel around the world! But I might have to pay a lot of taxes!

Ted's Introductory Paragraph

Winning a million dollars would change my life in many ways. Suddenly I would be able to buy all those things I had only dreamed about. But becoming rich might also make my life and my relationships much more complicated.

1. Does the first sentence say something about the good and bad effects of winning a million dollars?

   Cathy's _____ Ted's _____

2. Do the writer's preview sentences come from the group names? (You can find Cathy's and Ted's group names on pages 84–85.)

   Cathy's _____ Ted's _____

3. Are there any unnecessary or misleading sentences?

   Cathy's _____ Ted's _____

4. Which paragraph gives you the best idea of what the paper will be about? _____

Discussion

1. **Cathy's:** No. She only talks about how excited she would be if she won the money.

   Ted's: Yes. He says it would change a person's life in many ways. This indicates both positive and negative effects.

2. **Cathy's:** No. Cathy does not mention "Bad Effects—Personal" or "Bad Effects—From Outside World." She does mention some of the ideas from "Good Effects," but preview sentences should state main ideas, not examples.

   Ted's: Yes. Ted mentions that he could buy many things and that his life and relationships would be affected.

3. **Cathy's:** Yes. Cathy has told us only details, not main ideas. This is misleading because we don't know what to expect from her paper.

   Ted's: No. Ted's paragraph is on topic.

4. Ted's paragraph is more direct, includes all his main ideas, clearly states what his paper will be about, and is the better paragraph.

STEP 6 Review
Writing the Body

Summary

▼ The name of each group becomes the topic sentence of each paragraph. The ideas listed under each group name become the sentences for each paragraph.

Extra Practice (Help)

When you write a paragraph in the body of your composition, it is important to stick to the program your topic sentence announces. This section treats a common problem—getting away from the topic sentence—and suggests a way to help solve it, **coaching**. Coaching is having someone else read your paper and offer suggestions. It can be anyone—friend, relative, tutor, teacher—who will give you some serious feedback.

Ted had written a very strong introductory paragraph for his composition on the effects of winning a million dollars. Read Ted's introductory paragraph on page 88.

Ted used his first preview sentence, which was based on his group named "Things I Could Buy," to make the topic sentence for the first paragraph of the body. But then he got off his topic. Read Ted's paragraph.

Ted's First Body Paragraph

If I won a million dollars, I could buy almost everything I ever wanted! I could really impress my friends with the new sports car I would buy. I would take my friends all over town and also out to the lake. We would play our favorite music loud and have a great time. Of course, my parents wouldn't like that idea at all. They want me to stick around the house all the time.

Ted showed his paragraph to his good friend Richard. Below is the conversation Ted and Richard had about Ted's writing.

Richard: Ted, you really got off to a great start. You told me just what you were going to write about. I was ready to hear about all the wonderful things you were going to buy. You said you would buy a sports car, then you started talking about what you would do with the car, and how your parents would react. I wanted to hear about what else you were going to buy, but you never told me.

Ted: Well, I can see your point. I guess I got so excited thinking about the sports car that I forgot everything else.

Richard: Did your idea list have other things you would like to buy?

Ted: Yes, I had lots of things—land, gold, expensive clothes, a VCR, a compact disc player, and nice things for my family and friends.

Richard: Why don't you go back and use some of those ideas to rewrite your paragraph?

Ted: I'll do that.

Ted's Improved Paragraph

If I won a million dollars, I could buy almost everything I ever wanted! First, I would buy the sleekest little red sports car I could find. My friends and I would have a great time riding around in it. We would listen to music full blast on the compact disc player it would have. We would cruise out in the country, and I would scout out land to buy. I would also buy gold and a VCR. I might even get some nice things for my mom and dad (if they were nice to me).

Ted had improved his paragraph. His new paragraph develops the stated topic—the things Ted would buy—without reading like a list.

STEP 7 Review
Writing the Conclusion

Summary

▼ A concluding paragraph should do three things:

1. tie up your composition

2. relate to the points in the introductory paragraph

3. provide a strong, clear ending to your composition

▼ Don't simply restate the points made in your introductory paragraph. Use opinions or solutions to keep your readers' interest.

Extra Practice (Help)

Read the introductory paragraph and concluding paragraph Ted wrote for the composition about winning a million dollars.

Ted's Introductory Paragraph

Winning a million dollars would change my life in many ways. Suddenly I would be able to buy all those things I had only dreamed about. But becoming rich might also make my life and my relationships much more complicated.

Ted's Concluding Paragraph

So how would winning a million dollars change my life? I would probably really enjoy driving that expensive little sports car, but I would have to take good care of it. You have to check the oil just like any other car. Also, I would try not to become a snob! After all, one day I might spend all my money and just be a regular person again. I would try to invest my money and make more money. That way I wouldn't ever have to work again! Wish me luck!

This is not a good concluding paragraph. It rambles and jumps from one idea to another. It would be much better if it were planned out and organized. It doesn't relate closely enough to the introductory paragraph to sum up the composition effectively. It tries to keep the readers' interest, but it adds distracting new information.

Ted revised his concluding paragraph to make it stronger. Read his new concluding paragraph.

Ted's Revised Conclusion

So how would winning a million dollars change my life? I would really enjoy all my wonderful new possessions. However, becoming wealthy would probably create some difficulties. My friends might be jealous or manipulative. My parents might try to control me. I would have many more decisions to make. I certainly wouldn't turn it down, but winning a million dollars might give me a headache.

Ted's new concluding paragraph is much better. It sums up the points he first brought up in his introductory paragraph. It ties everything together and convinces the reader that he has made valid points.

STEP 8 Review
Improving Your Composition

Summary

▼ When you evaluate your composition, ask yourself three questions:

1. Did I stick to the topic?

2. Did I provide enough support for my topic?

3. How can I improve my composition?

Extra Practice (Help)

Evaluating your composition means rereading it and checking it against the topic and the ideas in the lists. Look again at Ted's topic and one of his groups of ideas.

> **Topic:** Discuss the good effects and the bad effects of winning a million dollars.

How It Would Affect Me

difficult decisions
use it to make more money
miserable if I ran out of money
become lazy and a snob
unsure of why others want to be friends

When Ted evaluated his composition, he found a paragraph that needed work. Several sentences were off the topic. He also had left out an idea that was on his list. Read Ted's paragraph about how winning a million dollars would affect him.

Ted's Original Paragraph

Winning that much money would have many affects on me. I would have to make many difficult decisions. I would try to invest my money wisely so that I could make more money and always be rich. My friend's uncle is rich. He lives in a huge mansion with a swimming pool. But what if I made bad decisions and lost the money? I would be miserable! Or what if I was successful in making more money and could lead a life of luxury? I might become lazy and a snob, then no one would like me!

Ted decided to take out the unneeded sentences and to add several sentences about the additional idea. Read Ted's revised paragraph.

Ted's Revised Paragraph

Winning that much money would have many affects on me. I would have to make many difficult decisions. I would try to invest my money wisely so that I could make more money and always be rich. But what if I made bad decisions and lost the money? I would be miserable! Or what if I was successful in making more money and could lead a life of luxury? I might become lazy and a snob, then no one would like me! I might also have to worry about why others want to be friends with me. Do they really like me, or are they pretending to like me because I have money?

Ted's revised paragraph follows the topic and includes the ideas he had listed in his group about how winning a million dollars would affect him.

Practicing for the Test

Know the Steps

Let's review what you have learned in this writing book. Read the chart below.

P	Plan	Step 1 Read the writing assignment.
		Step 2 List your ideas.
O	Organize	Step 3 Group your ideas. Name each group.
		Step 4 Expand your groups. Put your groups in order.
W	Write	Step 5 Write the introduction.
		Step 6 Write the body.
		Step 7 Write the conclusion.
E	Evaluate	Step 8 Evaluate your composition.
R	Revise	Make the changes that are needed.

Now your job is to practice the steps you have learned until they become automatic. Just as with anything else, the only way to become good at writing is to practice. You will become a good writer more quickly if you practice in a systematic way. This chapter has more practice writing assignments for you to choose from and write about. It also contains a Writing Guide. The Writing Guide will help you remember the steps to good writing as you work with the topic you have chosen. And it will help you practice your writing.

Fill in the Writing Guide as you write your first practice composition. Follow each step carefully. If you forget what a step means, look back and read about it again. Be sure to check the Summaries and models in the A part of each step.

Writing Under a Time Limit

Once you are comfortable with the POWER writing process, you need to consider one more thing. Most essay tests have a time limit. You may be allowed only 45 minutes for your writing test. So it is important to practice your writing with that time limit in mind.

Remember if you take a little more time to plan and organize carefully, you will need less time to write, evaluate, and revise. The writing will flow. You will know where you're going. The time chart below suggests a way of dividing the time you spend on each step.

Timed POWER	
Planning:	10 minutes
Organizing:	10 minutes
Writing:	15 minutes
Evaluating:	5 minutes
Revising:	5 minutes

You will notice that in this chart 20 minutes out of the 45 minutes is spent planning and organizing. Every person is different. You may find yourself spending less time on one step and more time on another. But keep in mind the importance of planning and organizing.

Are you ready? Choose a practice writing assignment (pages 99–100) and work through the Writing Guide (pages 101–111) using the time chart suggestions. When you've finished your first composition, choose a second writing assignment and repeat the process. Keep choosing topics and writing compositions. Time yourself until you feel you can really do a good job writing a composition within the 45 minute time limit. Each section of the Writing Guide contains suggested time limits for each step.

Choose a Topic

Read the writing assignments on pages 99 and 100. Choose one of the writing assignments to write about. Write your composition on pages 101 to 110. These pages are a Writing Guide that will help you remember the POWER Steps. Time yourself as you become more confident in using the POWER Program.

1. Recently, the city of Los Angeles started holding school all year long. Other communities are thinking of trying this plan. A typical schedule would be 9 weeks of instruction, then 3 weeks of vacation. Some people feel that such a schedule helps students learn more effectively. Others feel that the long summer vacation is important for student jobs and family life. They feel that both teachers and students will "burn out" under a heavy school schedule with only short breaks.

   In a composition of about 200 words, discuss the possible effects of a year-round school schedule. Consider the effects on both teachers and students. You may wish to deal with the good effects, the bad effects, or both.

2. We are pursued by ads and commercials on television, radio, and billboards, and in every magazine we buy. Advertising can keep us informed about new products and ideas that improve our lives. At the same time, advertising can confuse us until it is hard to make intelligent choices, and we end up wasting both time and money.

   Write a composition of about 200 words describing the effects of advertising in our lives. You may describe the good effects, or the bad effects, or both. Be specific. Use examples to support your view.

3. Many students are greatly tempted to drop out of school as soon as they legally may do so. When work is easy to get, it often seems a waste of time to continue attending school if you could be earning your own way and even helping your family. On the other hand, a high school diploma can open the door to more choices in the future.

   Write a composition of about 200 words concerning what one needs to consider when deciding whether or not to stay in school. Be specific. Use examples to support your view.

4. Extracurricular activities are generally recognized as an important part of school life. Many students who do not do well in their studies gain success and confidence in these activities. However, fearing that studies are often neglected, a number of schools do not allow students to take part in sports and other activities unless they have a passing grade in every academic subject.

   In a composition of about 200 words, give your opinion of the academic grade requirement for taking part in school sports and other activities. You may deal with the good effects, the bad effects, or both. Be specific. Use examples to support your view.

5. Many students have after-school jobs. They are able to earn considerable money as well as gain work experience for the future. However, many of these jobs require long hours on weekdays and nights as well as weekends. Long work hours leave little time for family, homework, and other school activities.

   Write a composition of about 200 words describing the effect you think after-school jobs have on students. You may talk about the good or bad effects or both. Be specific. Use examples to support your view.

Set Your Watch and Go

POWER Writing Guide

Choose one of the practice writing assignments on pages 99–100. Use this POWER Writing Guide to help you practice writing a composition using the eight POWER Steps. Use the stopwatches to help you keep track of your time.

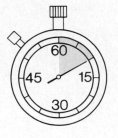

> **TIME REMINDER**
> Allow 10 minutes to do Steps 1 and 2.

Step 1 Read the writing assignment.

▼ Write the topic you have chosen below.

_____

_____

_____

Step 2 List your ideas.

▼ List everything you can think of that might be included in a composition on this topic.

_____ _____

_____ _____

_____ _____

_____ _____

_____ _____

Step 3 Group your ideas.
Name each group.

> **TIME REMINDER**
> Allow 10 minutes to do Steps 3 and 4.

▼ Put all the ideas that go together in the same group. Make three groups. If some things don't fit in a group, leave them out.

▼ Give each group a name that will cover all of the ideas in that group.

Group Name   **Group Name**   **Group Name**

_____   _____   _____

_____   _____   _____

_____   _____   _____

Ideas   **Ideas**   **Ideas**

_____   _____   _____

_____   _____   _____

_____   _____   _____

_____   _____   _____

_____   _____   _____

_____   _____   _____

_____   _____   _____

_____   _____   _____

Step 4 Expand your groups.
Put your groups in order.

▼ Arrange your groups from the least important to the most important.

Order of Groups
This group will be
number _____.

Group Name

_____

Ideas   Expanded Ideas

_____   _____

_____   _____

_____   _____

_____   _____

_____   _____

_____   _____

_____   _____

_____   _____

_____   _____

_____   _____

_____   _____

_____   _____

_____   _____

_____   _____

Order of Groups
This group will be
number _____.

Group Name

_____

Ideas

Expanded Ideas

_____   _____

_____   _____

_____   _____

_____   _____

_____   _____

_____   _____

_____   _____

_____   _____

_____   _____

_____   _____

_____   _____

_____   _____

_____   _____

_____   _____

_____   _____

_____   _____

_____   _____

_____   _____

Order of Groups
This group will be
number _____ .

Group Name

_____

Ideas

Expanded Ideas

_____   _____

_____   _____

_____   _____

_____   _____

_____   _____

_____   _____

_____   _____

_____   _____

_____   _____

_____   _____

_____   _____

_____   _____

_____   _____

_____   _____

_____   _____

_____   _____

_____   _____

_____   _____

_____   _____

Step 5 Write the introduction.

> **TIME REMINDER**
> Allow 15 minutes to do Steps 5, 6, and 7.

▼ Look back at Step 1 and read the topic. Turn the topic into your topic sentence, the first sentence of your introductory paragraph.

▼ Look back at Step 4 and read the names of your groups. Use your group names to write the preview sentences that support your topic sentence.

Introductory Paragraph

_____

_____

_____

_____

_____

_____

_____

_____

_____

_____

_____

Step 6 Write the body.

▼ Use your expanded groups to write each paragraph in the body. For each paragraph, turn the group name into the topic sentence. Turn the ideas into supporting sentences.

First Paragraph (in the body)

_____

_____

_____

_____

_____

_____

Second Paragraph

_____

_____

_____

_____

_____

_____

_____

_____

Third Paragraph

_____

_____

_____

_____

_____

_____

_____

_____

_____

Step 7 Write the conclusion.

▼ Reword the introductory paragraph with emphasis on your conclusions.

_____

_____

_____

_____

_____

_____

_____

_____

_____

Step 8 Read your composition.
Make the changes that are needed.

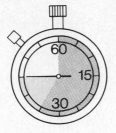

TIME REMINDER
Allow 10 minutes to do Step 8.

▼ Read your composition to see if you stayed on the topic, supported your topic, and wrote correctly. (Use the Writer's Handbook on pages 112–122 for help.)

▼ Add any needed explanations or examples. Delete any irrelevant sentences. Make any needed corrections.

▼ Rewrite your composition.

_____

_____

_____

_____

_____

_____

_____

_____

_____

_____

_____

_____

_____

Now you are ready to try the other writing assignments. Look back at the practice assignments on pages 99 and 100. Pick another topic to write about on your own paper. Follow the POWER Steps carefully. Use the review section on pages 80 to 95 for more help.

The more you practice, the more likely it will be that the POWER Steps will become automatic for you. When that happens—when you can take the POWER Steps and write a satisfactory composition—you'll have the POWER you need to pass any writing test.

Use the questions below to help you keep track of your progress.

Practice Compositions

TOPICS

a. Did I understand the topic and the instructions?

1	2	3	4	5

b. Did I list my ideas?

1	2	3	4	5

c. Did I group my ideas and name each group?

1	2	3	4	5

d. Did I expand my groups and put my groups in order?

1	2	3	4	5

e. Did I write my introductory paragraph from the topic and the names of my groups?

1	2	3	4	5

f. Did I write the paragraphs in the body from my groups and lists?

1	2	3	4	5

g. Did I write my conclusion from the topic and end my essay with a punch?

1	2	3	4	5

h. Did I evaluate and revise my composition to make it the best it could be?

1	2	3	4	5

i. Did I complete my composition in the time limit?

1	2	3	4	5

Writer's Handbook

Sentence Fragments

A sentence is a group of words that expresses a complete thought. A sentence must have a **subject** and a **verb**. The subject tells who or what did the action. The verb is a word that shows action or state of being. Read these sentences in which the subject and verb have been marked with an **s** and a **v**.

Many people like ice cream.   Oak trees grow very tall.
       s   v   s   v

A **fragment** is a group of words that does not express a complete thought, but that has a period at the end. A fragment is usually an error.

A fragment can be corrected in two ways. One way is to add the fragment to a complete sentence. The other way is to add words to the fragment to make it a sentence.

Notice that in the examples below, the fragment, or error, has been underlined.

Fragment: Some people have unusual pets. Like lizards and snakes.

Correction: Some people have unusual pets. Lizards and snakes are two kinds of unusual pets.

Fragment: After finishing the project. The workers went home.

Correction: After finishing the project, the workers went home.

Practice

Correct these fragments by adding words to make complete sentences. There is more than one way to correct these. Your answer is correct if you have a complete thought.

Fragment: Working hard for a living.

Correction: I am working hard for a living.

Correction: Working hard for a living, I get tired by evening.

1. Getting out of the habit of smoking.

_____

_____

2. Going to the movies this evening.

_____

_____

3. After the Super Bowl Game.

_____

_____

4. The Dallas Cowboys and the New York Giants.

_____

_____

5. After playing baseball for several years.

_____

_____

6. Like sports and hobbies.

_____

_____

Run-On Sentences

A **run-on** sentence is an error. It is two sentences that are put together as if they were only one sentence. A run-on has two subjects and two verbs. It expresses two complete thoughts.

There are two types of run-ons. One has two complete thoughts joined by a comma. The other has two complete thoughts joined with no punctuation at all. Read the examples of run-ons given below. The subjects and verbs are underlined.

There are two ways to correct run-ons. One way is to put a period between the two parts. The other way is to use a comma and a joining word (conjunction) such as **and, but, or, nor, so, for,** or **yet**.

Run-on: Many children enjoy summer vacation, these same children may enjoy school, too.

Run-on: Many children enjoy summer vacation these same children may enjoy school, too.

Correction: Many children enjoy summer vacation. These same children may enjoy school, too.

Correction: Many children enjoy summer vacation, but these same children may enjoy school, too.

Run-on: Some people fear burglars, these people may have big guard dogs for protection.

Run-on: Some people fear burglars these people may have big guard dogs for protection.

Correction: Some people fear burglars. These people may have big guard dogs for protection.

Correction: Some people fear burglars, so these people may have big guard dogs for protection.

Practice

Correct the following run-on sentences in one of two ways.
Either separate the two thoughts by adding a period and a
capital letter, or add a comma and a conjunction.

1. The team had lost the game the players were not happy.

   _____

   _____

2. Most children do not go to school all year they have
   vacation in the summer.

   _____

   _____

3. My mother likes movies she does not like television very
   much.

   _____

   _____

4. My friend lived in Georgia she liked the warm weather.

   _____

   _____

5. Some people have many pets others have no pets at all.

   _____

   _____

6. I worked hard at my job I did not get a raise.

   _____

   _____

Capitalization

1. Always capitalize the first word of a sentence.

    Tomorrow is Saturday.

2. Always capitalize *I*.

    Juan and I are brothers.

3. Always capitalize the names of people, groups, nationalities, places, and events.

Dolly Parton	New England
the Democrats	Elm Street
French people	the Watermelon Festival

4. Always capitalize the days of the week, months of the year, and holidays. Do not capitalize the seasons.

Tuesday	April	Christmas	winter

5. Always capitalize the first word and all important words in titles of songs, magazines, books, newspapers, movies, and television programs. Do not capitalize prepositions or articles within a title.

"The Star Spangled Banner"	*Time* magazine
The Adventures of Tom Sawyer	*Chicago Tribune*

6. Always capitalize *President* when referring to the President of a country. Capitalize other titles only when they are used before a name, but not when they come after a name or are used alone.

President Kennedy	the President of the U.S.
Dr. John Wilson	the doctors at the clinic

Practice

In the sentences below, circle the words that should be capitalized.

1. many kids today watch cartoons like the "smurfs" on saturday mornings.

2. the american pioneers took many months to travel to the west in their covered wagons.

3. today i can drive my car from new york to san francisco in less than a week.

4. an article in the *new york times* reported that dr. spock thinks young children should use their imaginations instead of watching television.

5. school children have vacation in the winter months of november and december for the thanksgiving and christmas holidays.

6. do children still read *the adventures of huckleberry finn* and watch reruns of "the waltons"?

7. the humane society takes in stray animals.

8. if the boston city council lets the boston symphony orchestra play in the park, should michael jackson be allowed to perform there, too?

9. i have appointments to see my doctor, my lawyer, and my dentist, dr. james street.

10. i hope to travel to france someday to see the arch of triumph and the eiffel tower.

Punctuation

Commas are like road signs. They show the reader how to follow the meaning of a sentence.

1. Put a comma between each item in a series.

   The recipe calls for potatoes, onions, and cheese.

2. Put commas both between and after the parts of dates and addresses.

   On November 22, 1963, President Kennedy was assassinated in Dallas, Texas.

3. Put a comma between the two complete sentences joined by a conjunction.

   The young children played on the beach, and the older ones swam in the lake.

Another form of punctuation is the **apostrophe**.

1. Use an apostrophe to show ownership. Where you put the apostrophe depends upon whether you are talking about *one* or *more than one* person or thing.

Only One	**More Than One**
my doctor's house	doctors' houses
(one doctor)	(a few doctors)

2. Use an apostrophe to show letters have been omitted in a contraction.

   do not . . . don't   we have . . . we've   let us . . . let's

A. Practice

Put commas where they belong in the following sentences.

1. Radio television and movies were all invented in the last 100 years.

2. The hills are steep and the valleys are deep.

3. Happiness may come from good health work you enjoy and a loving family.

4. I work for the city but my brother works for the state.

5. Her new address is 200 W. Maple Smithville Ohio.

6. Our last meeting was Tuesday September 8 1986 at 6:30 p.m.

B. Practice

In each of the following sentences, circle the words with the apostrophe in the correct place.

7. I went over to my (friend's/friends') house after work, but he (wa'snt/wasn't) there.

8. (Don't/Do'nt) expect your (car's/cars') engine to stay in good condition without regular maintenance.

9. (Theyr'e/They're) interested in finding out whether the two (program's/programs') ratings improved this year.

10. My (lawyer's/lawyers') office is very large for just one person.

11. The (worker's/workers') tools were left on their benches during the fire drill.

Spelling

1. Words that sound alike but are not spelled alike are sometimes confused. Pay attention to what each word means. Remember the spelling and meaning of each word. Look at the sound-alike words below.

    its—it's   their—there—they're
    your—you're   to—too—two

    The cat licks **its** long fur. (shows ownership)
    It's a simple idea. (contraction for *it is*)

    I'm sorry I hurt **your** feelings. (shows ownership)
    Tell me where **you're** going. (contraction for *you are*)

    Their plan was confusing. (shows ownership)
    They're buying a new car. (contraction for *they are*)
    The car is over **there**. (tells where)

    She went **to** the concert. (tells where)
    She wanted ice cream, **too**. (also)
    Two heads are better than one. (a number)

2. If a word—such as **ride** or **smile**—ends in a consonant and an **e**, you usually drop the **e** when adding an ending that begins with a vowel.

    rid¢ + ing = riding   smil¢ + ed = smiled

3. If a one-syllable word—such as **get** or **run**—is in a consonant-vowel-consonant pattern (**r-u-n**), double the final
    c-v-c
    consonant when adding an ending that begins with a vowel.

    get + ing = getting   run + ing = running

A. Practice

In the sentences below, circle the sound-alike words that are spelled correctly according to the meaning they have in the sentence.

1. The nicest part of (their/they're/there) new house is (its/it's) big front porch.

2. The solution to (your/you're) problem depends upon what (their/they're/there) boss says.

3. Yesterday the committee made (its/it's) decision to allow members to bring (their/they're/there) husbands or wives, (to/too/two).

4. If (your/you're) relatives want to visit you during the holidays, you can take (to/too/two) weeks of vacation.

5. (Its/It's) easy to see from (your/you're) red eyes that (your/you're) tired today.

6. (Their/They're/There) complaining that (its/it's) (to/too/two) cold in (their/they're/there).

B. Practice

Write the correct spelling for each of the following words + suffixes.

7. drop + ing _____   8. hope + ing _____

9. hide + ing _____   10. stop + ed _____

11. date + ing _____   12. give + ing _____

13. rob + ed _____   14. swim + ing _____

Writer's Handbook Answer Key

Sentence Fragments (pages 112–113)

1–6 Answers will vary. Possible answers: **1.** Getting out of the habit of smoking is not easy. **2.** I am going to the movies this evening. **3.** After the Super Bowl Game, we will eat dinner. **4.** The Dallas Cowboys and the New York Giants will play football on Sunday. **5.** After playing baseball for several years, I became interested in football. **6.** I like sports and hobbies.

Run-on Sentences (pages 114–115)

1. The team had lost the game. The players were not happy. **or** The team had lost the game, so the players were not happy. **2.** Most children do not go to school all year. They have vacation in the summer. **or** Most children do not go to school all year, for they have vacation in the summer. **3.** My mother likes movies. She does not like television very much. **or** My mother likes movies, but she does not like television very much. **4.** My friend lived in Georgia. She liked the warm weather. **or** My friend lived in Georgia, and she liked the warm weather. **5.** Some people have many pets. Others have no pets at all. **or** Some people have many pets, but others have no pets at all. **6.** I worked hard at my job. I did not get a raise. **or** I worked hard at my job, but I did not get a raise.

Capitalization (pages 116–117)

1. Many, "Smurfs," Saturday **2.** The, American, West **3.** Today, I, New York, San Francisco **4.** An, *New York Times*, Dr. Spock **5.** School, November, December, Thanksgiving, Christmas **6.** Do, *The Adventures of Huckleberry Finn*, "The Waltons" **7.** The Humane Society **8.** If, Boston City Council, Boston Symphony Orchestra, Michael Jackson **9.** I, Dr. James Street **10.** I, France, Arch of Triumph, Eiffel Tower

Punctuation (pages 118–119)

A. 1. Radio, television, and **2.** steep, and **3.** health, work . . . enjoy, and **4.** city, but **5.** Maple, Smithville, Ohio **6.** Tuesday, September 8, 1986, at   **B. 7.** friend's, wasn't **8.** Don't, car's **9.** They're, programs' **10.** lawyer's **11.** workers'

Spelling (pages 120–121)

A. 1. their, its **2.** your, their **3.** its, their, too **4.** your, two **5.** It's, your, you're **6.** They're, it's, too, there **B. 7.** dropping **8.** hoping **9.** hiding **10.** stopped **11.** dating **12.** giving **13.** robbed **14.** swimming

Answers to Practice Exercises

STEP 1 Answers to Practice Exercises on pages 11–13

1. **Topic** explain your own opinion of skateboards
   Instructions In a composition of about 200 words . . . Be specific. Give examples to support your view.

2. **Topic** stating whether you think it is better to stay in one place or to move often and live different places
   Instructions Write a composition of about 200 words . . . Be specific. Give examples to support your view.

3. **Topic** stating whether you think football players are paid too much or not
   Instructions Write a composition of about 200 words . . . Explain your view. Give specific examples about football and about other kinds of work.
   Check what you wrote. Did you restate the topic? Did you include all the instructions?

STEP 2 Answers to Practice Exercises on pages 20-22

1. Some additional ideas: good way to travel, problem finding culverts to do tricks in, good activity for friends, tricks can be dangerous, trick contests can be fun and challenging, status symbol.

2. These ideas are probably off the topic: movies, books, music. Possible additional ideas: leave relatives, takes awhile to make new friends, miss old friends.

3. Look at your idea list. Ask yourself these questions:
   ▼ How long is my list?
   ▼ How strong is my list?
   ▼ Is every idea about the topic?
   ▼ Are there any other ideas I could add?

STEP 3   Answers to Practice Exercises on pages 28–30

1. **Good Aspects—Health** good exercise, develop balance
    Good Aspects—Self-Concept good way to travel, good
    activity for friends to do together, trick contests can be fun
    and challenging, gives kids goals to strive for, status symbol
    Problems chance of injury, problem finding safe culverts
    to do tricks in, tricks can be dangerous
    Note: The list can be grouped in other ways. Compare
    your groups with the ones here. If your groups are
    different, ask yourself if your groups make sense.

2. Your group names may be different but should give the
    same general ideas. These are possible answers:
    Group A Benefits of Staying in One Place
    Group B Benefits of Moving Often
    Group C Difficulties of Moving Often

3. Your groups and ideas may vary widely. Look at your groups
    and their names. Ask yourself these questions:
    ▼ Do all the ideas in each group have something in common?
    ▼ Does the name of each group really tell the main idea
       of that group?

    Here is one possible grouping:
    Deserve Large Salaries—Physical Reasons takes much skill
    (only the best make it), possibility of serious injury, limited
    number of playing years, very physically demanding
    Deserve Large Salaries—Entertainment Reasons provides
    excitement and enjoyment to many, produces much income—
    players deserve their share
    Do Not Deserve Such Large Salaries only play part of the
    year, shorter hours than most jobs, some players just sit on the
    bench but make hundreds of thousands of dollars, other
    people have more essential jobs (police, fire fighters, teachers)
    but are paid much less

STEP 4　Answers to Practice Exercises on pages 36–37

1. Your answers may vary widely from the ones below. This is only one possible solution.

   2 Group A: Good Aspects—Health
   1 good exercise— heart, leg muscles
   2 develop balance—improves coordination

   3 Group B: Good Aspects—Self-Concept
   1 good way to travel—cheap, fun
   2 good activity for friends to do together—active
   4 trick contests can be fun and challenging
   5 gives kids goals to strive for— practice
   3 status symbol—based on skill

   1 Group C: Problems
   3 chance of injury—scrapes, sprains, broken bones
   1 problem finding safe culverts to do tricks in—kids sometimes skateboard in dangerous places
   2 tricks can be dangerous

   Your answers will depend on how you ordered the ideas. Here is one possible solution.

   Group 1 (weakest): Problems
   problem finding safe culverts to do tricks in
   tricks can be dangerous
   chance of injury

   Group 2 (middle): Good Aspects—Health
   good exercise
   develop balance

   Group 3 (strongest): Good Aspects—Self-Concept
   good way to travel
   good activity for friends to do together
   status symbol
   trick contests can be fun and challenging
   gives kids goals to strive for

   Your lists may be in a different order. Just be sure they are in an order (weakest to strongest) that will work for you.

STEP 5 Answers to Practice Exercises on pages 44–49

1. **Topic sentence** Regular exercise is good for your general health.

2. **Preview sentences** Skateboards can cause problems if they are used carelessly. But if you use skateboards wisely, they can help your health and your self-concept.

3. a. What are the advantages of shopping at a large supermarket?
b. No. It is a question.
c. This is a question that many people ask. This paper is going to answer this question because so many people have asked it. There must be reasons or why would we shop there? I prefer to shop there myself. d. no e. no f. yes
Possible topic sentence There are many advantages of shopping in large supermarkets that sell a variety of products.
Possible preview sentences These stores make shopping very convenient. You can also save money by shopping in these stores.
Analyze Your Paragraph Check your topic sentence to see if it states your position clearly. Make sure your preview sentences tell how you will approach the topic. An interesting and direct paragraph will keep your reader's attention.

4. Possible introductory paragraph:
   Although there are advantages and disadvantages to both, I prefer being settled in one place to moving often. Moving often causes many exciting changes, but it also creates many difficulties. Living in one place provides many benefits.

5. Possible introductory paragraph:
   Football players make very large salaries, and I believe they deserve the money. Some people think it is unfair that they are so well paid. I think that football demands such physical skill and provides entertainment to so many people that the players earn their money.

STEP 6   Answers to Practice Exercises on pages 55–56

1. Possible second paragraph:

    Owning a car would mean that I would have more
    responsibility. I could take pride in owning my very own
    car. I would take good care of it. I would wash my car
    often, and maybe even learn to work on it. If I had a car, I
    could get a job. I would have transportation to and from
    work. Then I would learn the responsibility of keeping a
    job, and also of spending my money wisely.

2. Possible third paragraph:

    The best effect of owning a car would be the freedom it
    would give me. I could do so many things I can't do now. I
    could go out for rides in the country. I could visit my
    friends and take them places. I could give my best friend a
    ride to school, and we could go shopping on our own. I
    wouldn't have to ask other people for rides or ask my
    parents if I could borrow their car. Having a car of my
    own would give me freedom and independence.

STEP 7   Answers to Practice Exercises on pages 64–67

1. This is an example. Yours may be very different.

    Why is skateboarding controversial? Some people form
    a bad impression of the sport because they see kids being
    daredevils. They hear about skateboard injuries and assume
    the worst. Skateboarding is no more dangerous than any other
    sport. It is good for your health and your self-concept. Kids are
    encouraged to exercise, set goals, and strive for those goals.
    Skateboarding is a healthy, fun activity.

2. This is an example. Yours may be very different.

    People in our society today are very mobile. Although it
    would be exciting to explore new places, I think there are
    many disadvantages to moving often. In the past, families
    were surrounded by friends, neighbors, and relatives. I think
    we would be better off if we still had that sense of belonging.

STEP 8   Answers to Practice Exercises on pages 76–77

1. There are several places where Jim doesn't stick to his topic. He should take out the following sentences.
   1st paragraph: I own a car and so does my brother. We like to race at the local race track in amateur contests.
   2nd paragraph: One great group is Van Halen. I have three of their tapes.
   4th paragraph: Bus riding is okay. My brother and I rode the bus everywhere before we got our cars.
   Now every sentence supports his topic.

2. When Jim compared his composition to his idea list, he realized he hadn't written anything about vacations. He decided to revise the last part of his second paragraph. He rewrote the last sentence and made it two sentences.

   Revision: Another advantage to having a car is that you can take vacations in it. A car makes it easier to carry things, too—from luggage for a vacation to groceries from the supermarket.

   Jim also decided that the organization of the body could be better. Since he thought the advantages of owning a car are more important than the disadvantages, he decided to put the paragraph on advantages after the paragraph on disadvantages. This would follow the weaker-to-stronger rule of organization.

   You may have approached the revision a little differently. Just be sure that you took out the sentences that weren't on topic and added the ideas that had been left out. Feel free to make any other revisions that will further improve the composition.